ORDINARY
GRAVITY

GARY
LARK

ORDINARY GRAVITY

GARY LARK

Airlie Press
PORTLAND OREGON
2019

Airlie Press is supported by book sales, by contributions to the press
from its supporters, and by the work donated by
all the poet-editors of the press.

P.O. Box 82653
Portland, OR 97282
www.airliepress.org

email: editors@airliepress.org

Cover and Book Design: Beth Ford, Glib Communications & Design

First Edition
ISBN: 978-0-9895799-8-8
Library of Congress Control Number: 2018965629

Printed in the United States of America

CONTENTS

IV

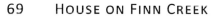

V

FATHER'S PEOPLE

They lived up the rivers on patches of bottom land
and side hills growing gardens, eating venison.
Young men could start working in the woods at sixteen
earning a man's wages, hunt the clear cuts
and fish on streams where cougar and bear
were the only competitors.
The cut pushed further into the hills.
Log trucks replaced little rail spurs
hauling some of the most beautiful wood
the world ever produced to the mills.
But there were places up the shaded river reaches
where the stillness that wasn't still
and the silence that wasn't silent
crept into the listener and wrung his mind
like Monday wash. In that place of no human sound
and primeval wonder it was like standing
on God's front porch, seeing a balance
and meaning of things that couldn't be spoken—
the murmur and crash of a small river
getting bigger as it slips and carves
through stands of virgin fir,
nursed and coached by alder and maple
along its banks, folds of land
untroubled but by deer hooves
and marten claws, all strewn and buckled
by plate tectonics and ice-age maneuvers,
seeds and sea bringing forth the day.
The listener would know that he was blessed
by something beyond his knowing.
Sometimes he had an axe in his hand,
sometimes a fishing pole or rifle, but he knew
he needed forgiveness with every step.

NAVY BEANS AND BACON RIND

Rain wanders across the pasture.
Father is home, no overtime tonight.
Navy beans and bacon rind
and a plate of biscuits,
what more could I want?

A torrent pounds the roof.
I like the chewy resistance of the rind,
the smoky flavor.
Next week after payday
maybe ham.

The gray light slides away.
I lay a biscuit in the bowl
and pour in more beans,
plenty in the steam
if you want some.

SECOND WEEK OF SCHOOL

There are junker cars,
trash spilling from a tow wagon
and clusters of broken farm tools
strung between what used to be a fence
and the pasture road that runs
to a green snake river.

Dayson and his half-washed sister
dawdle on the way to school,
blowing snot and pitching rocks
at swallow nests under the eaves of an old shed.
The birds left after other assaults
so all that's left are the weeks
of hard daubing dried to the shingles and beams,
a September rain attempts to cover it all.

I ride my rattling orange Western Flyer by,
knowing them as the Pratts
who live down the gravel road
on a dirt patch my parents describe as unworked—
that if there was any elbow grease applied
would yield the corn and berries and squash,
rabbits and chickens as ours does.

At school, between arithmetic
and work-up baseball games
the Pratts disappear.

THE SHARPER

The dusty 1934 Ford pickup
came up the drive
avoiding the axle busters
and eased to the side of the house.
A shingled wood frame
on the back housed his business.
Two grinding wheels, files,
a flat finishing stone
and a fold-up cot were evident
when he opened the door.
A dull knife in our house
would have insulted my father,
but The Sharper took care of saws
and scissors, loppers and hoes,
a scythe, an axe, so he stayed
an hour or two.
On good days he'd bring a wheel
down the ramp and set up in the yard.
Levering the stone wheel into position
he talked about fishing
or the weather or a neighbor's orchard
or a prize fight in Portland.
The Sharper started pedaling,
the wheel gaining speed
and us kids brought him
anything with an edge,
except the knives.

Sparks flew.
Then he began to wonder where stars come from,
and tell about the big flood on the Columbia
that cut through the Cascade mountains.
There's a two-headed sheep in The Dalles
and a gold nugget big as your fist
down on the Rogue River.
Saws, with their waggling teeth,
were meticulously filed.
He'd set a pencil on the row,
look at us and make his eyebrows dance.
His truck was old, he seemed ageless.
Sometime before I left home
he stopped coming.
He never made appointments
so there was just an absence,
all the dull saws and nicked hoes
needing a story.

LONG WALK

After breakfast we get Hector from the pen
and lead him up the road.
He follows on a slack rope
stopping for grass and to sniff.
He looks with caution
when we enter the big barn.
Our neighbor Labree, a dairy farmer,
has a block and tackle set up
near the cold room
down from the milking parlor.
A sour sweet silage smell drifts through.
Hector's head is barred in the stanchion
with molasses grain at his nose.

I am nine years old
and what is to happen is no secret.
Our Jersey cow births a calf
each year and we slaughter it.
They are named, treated well
and calmly walked to their destiny.
Father puts the rifle to Hector's forehead
and pulls the trigger. He drops.
Father and Labree hook the hind legs
and pull Hector up to man height.
Well whetted knives open the carcass.
Liver and heart wrapped to take with us.
The thirteen hundred pound calf that was Hector
will hang in the cool room for a week
before we come back and cut it
into steaks, roasts and stew meat,
grind hamburger.
In January, we suck fat marrow
from soup bones.

OLDEST GOOSE TO FALL FROM THE SKY

A small vee of geese circles the pasture,
Holsteins toward the river,
the dairyman bangs on our door.
"Hurry," he said. "Your shotgun."
Papa hands him the 16 gauge.
We go out in the yard
and watch as our neighbor
crouches along the fence line,
moves to a clutch of ash trees
and walks into the geese
near the pond. They rise.
He fires three times, two fall.
He brings back the gun
and one of the birds.
Mama, used to dressing chickens,
has it plucked, gutted
and into the oven in an hour.
It smells good roasting.
Papa carves and mama passes
the potatoes and carrots.
We chew and chew and chew.
"Who knew," Papa says,
"a hundred-year-old goose could fly."

LOWER RIVER ROAD

The roads are Stillworth, Decker and Frye,
Finnegan and Meade, Tuggsberry and Gilson.
So when you come to River Road
you know half the families who live there,
or the ones who have. And some of them
have seen you from their windows or fields;
for many, if not most, don't work out
at the mill or up in the timber, at least not much.
In fact it would be hard to say how they earn enough
to eat or buy a pair of boots every nine years.
So when you ask which way to the boat ramp
they lean on the gate or a shovel perusing
what's in your truck bed and the gear in your boat
with the practiced eye of a horse trader
seeing what they can get for that outboard
at the Saturday auction south of town.
Not that they are out-and-out thieves,
but they live for the moment
you drive back to town knowing
that somehow they have twisted your mind into a knot.

They have honed their skill on each other
for generations. The ones who couldn't cut it
sell insurance in town, a few go off to college
and never return, obviously a disgrace.
Some will watch as you back the boat
into the river, pull away from shore
and fish the channel on the other side.
Somebody different will be there
to see you unload your fish,
maybe ask what you were using,
although you never see any of them fishing.
You suspect they might use dynamite
or nets, perhaps after dark, just suspicions
that you feel guilty about having.
On the way home when you turn off River Road
onto Gilson you feel cobwebs still stuck
to your back and truck and boat, a near miss.

UNCLES

A braid of the Payette River runs
through the orchard canal.

Three brothers, great uncles and my grandfather,
sit around their sister's table.
One asks another, "Getting married again?"
"No, that didn't work out," the reply.
Everyone knows his first wife died
when a mine wall collapsed.
The second by falling off a horse
breaking her neck.
The third of some wasting disease.

I swam the canal from the neighbor's
that afternoon. It was swift enough
I didn't argue with it.

Another uncle talks about Ben,
the one who isn't there,
dying an "old man" at forty-five
when his ship was torpedoed
in WWII. He'd been ready to retire
when the war came around.
Nobody mentions his homosexuality.

The cherry orchard fits in a fold of hills,
old volcanic soil toward the top
and river loam at the bottom.

Talk swings around to lumber mills,
my father's profession, what's cut where
and how long they can keep it up,
that it's steady work, for now.
Grandfather smokes a Camel,
his life running across a West unfamiliar now,
herding sheep, a starvation farm,
building houses, drilling water wells.

They speak of their sister's good sense
to marry a man with an orchard.
She asks if they would like some pie.
He smokes his pipe.

WE DIDN'T TELL HIM WE WERE NEIGHBORS

Knight's land ran to the middle of the river.
Knight said so, had the deed from 1867
and by God meant to keep anyone
from trespassing on the rights
his grandfather had claimed.
It was good land, too, loam and leaves
laid down over thousands of years.
We had anchored where the north
and south forks come together
with other boats below a wide riffle.
Midmorning we discovered
we'd left the pee can at home.
So, with some trepidation,
we threw out the anchor rope float
and nudged the boat onto a spit of sand
just around the bend.
Quiet as we could, my brother and I
lined up to relieve ourselves.
Halfway through a voice came over the bank,
"You don't see me driving to town to piss on your lawn
do you? You haven't noticed me pissing on your porch
have you?"
We didn't answer, just finished fast as we could.
"I've a mind to blow those little peckers off."
He loomed above us, double-barreled shotgun
protruding from his hip.
We shoved off, started the motor and headed around the
bend.
"Next time I will, by God. You can count on it."
Then the BOOM! of the shotgun.
We both ducked involuntarily.
We reattached the anchor rope,
fished another hour and left before the next call.

THE GAME

Among this branch of McIntyres
the ones who didn't commit suicide
lived a long time.
I was in their house as much as my own,
went to school with Jamie.
His mom made pound cake for my birthdays.
We had a make-believe world
on the north side of the creek,
where bullies were dispatched
and magic made regular visits.
I found out about the suicide business
when Jamie's brother shot himself in the basement.
He was a sophomore.
The family, writhing like a wounded snake,
raged and hissed at each other.
His mom told me the calm times
were like waiting for a fire
to spring from somebody's head.
It was going to happen, but when?
Jamie seemed to grow up fast after that,
Baseball became more intense.
I had always been the better hitter,
he, the hotshot of the infield.
His father drilled a hole in a baseball,
attached a rope and we swung that for each other
until we both felt like we could hit anything.
I went to work in the mill after high school
but Jamie got a scholarship to a college upstate.
I think he's going to make it.
When he's home we watch his little brother
play the outfield.

GRANDPA CRAMER'S LAST SPEECH

Grandpa quit politics
on a stormy September night.
Before then he would get into it
down at Langley's store.
He would speechify on the church steps.
There was cussing and discussing
on the front porch.
He and his brother-in-law
would go round and round
late under a staring moon.
All through the politicking season
he would argue with a termite
if it crossed his path.

But that night, that wild night,
he was listening to a speech on the Philco
when a ball of lightning
rolled down the line,
along the house wires,
and blew up the radio.
I mean, it blew like a stick of dynamite:
smoking wires and tube glass,
veneer and wood chunks
scattered over the plank floor.
It was a sign.

When he was through cleaning up hot spots
Grandpa put down politics for good.
I mean, he wouldn't even stay in the same room
when the sides would start up.
Grandma liked that.

BRIDGE ACROSS

Faded green paint mostly covered
the iron bridgework that was trying to rust
and fall into the slick it spanned.
We crossed to fish the other side,
there always seemed to be a good hole
on the other side of any river we fished.
There was a little slipping-down house
on the side-hill just above us.
Squalling kids rooted and tumbled in the yard.
We had started fishing upriver a ways
thinking we were clear of them
when I saw him perched in the crotch of an oak.
Bobby was one of the slow kids,
not quite belonging in the shifting tides at school.
His blank stare hid the gyrations of his mind.
As we slid from hole to hole
Will and I glanced back.
Bobby followed.
Was he stalking? Was he lonely?
We caught our limit of trout by noon
and headed for the bridge.
Bobby skittered ahead of us.
I hollered to him.
He stopped, watched us approach.
I asked if he would like some fish.
He looked at me for a second
then off, anywhere else.
"No," he said.
I asked if he ever fished the river.
Again, "No".
Will and I recrossed the long reach,
Bobby watching us out of sight.

BEAST OF BURDEN

My father was one of the oxen
that pulled Northwest lumber mills
from the days of the Gyppo
and homegrown baron
to the era of international conglomerate.
In those early rough-cut days
the boss lived up the hill,
his kids went to the same school
and money spilled on the rainy slope
that ran from the view to the slough.
The little outfits got bought up,
squeezed out, bankrupted or burned.
Labor was still there at the gate
when the fiscal office
moved to Portland or Seattle
then Atlanta, and the money
sailed to a warm climate.
Father took early retirement
with half pension and bad lungs.
He was one of the lucky ones.

KEITH

No one from the ranch went to town to be born:
homestead natural selection.
Play in the creek, the haymow,
bring back a favorite horse biscuit
from the barn, little britches and dresses
dirty in half a day, children grew up free spirits
and tough, kind to the animals
they considered friends.
Spring water came from the tap
in the kitchen. One circuit
powered the house lights.
Keith was born in the south bedroom,
upstairs, overlooking the pasture.
He was set on a horse
before he could walk.
The Great Depression
accompanied his growing up.
He was six when he went with the men
to the high meadows to bring cattle
down for the winter.
At ten he drove the Case tractor
standing up to reach the pedals.
He was fourteen riding a motorcycle
with half-flat tires in the snow.
He was eighteen and a half
when they called him for Korea.
He did what they said, most of the time.

He knew how to live in the cold
and mud, but the stupidity
came one too many times.
On a day of hell, after weeks of hell,
Keith was told to go down the hill
into fire, literal and machine gun,
to certain death for no good cause
and he looked into the eyes
of the second lieutenant
and said, "My squad's not going."
He was joined by a few others.
Told he would be shot or court marshaled
he answered, "You'd better aim well."
He lived through that day
and the next, but before mustering out
was called before a row of men
in clean uniforms, decorations
heavy on their chests.
After hearing a dozen witnesses
he was allowed to go home.
There's a Silver Star in his sock drawer.
On a good day Keith sits a horse
on a hill with a hundred mile view.
On an arthritis day he rocks
on the porch and watches
his daughter and grandson
take hay to the cattle.

LESSON

The burning came,
a sudden snakebite
.22 rifle shot
square in the spine.
Twelve years old,
proud and stupid,
his buddy standing
between him and the sun.
"You dared me."

And he had.
Out plinking,
shooting birds
and stumps
by the creek
where it curls
back into the trees.
"You dared me."

And now the fire
started up from the gap
where feeling stops,
blazing up through his torso
into his twelve year old brain
showing him pictures
of wheelchairs, learning
to grab an unimagined life
from this terrible teacher.

SNAKE COUNTRY

Randal has the devil in him
some people say
because he handles snakes,
loves snakes,
lets them scooch all over him.
It's different than the folks up Peeler way
who keep a little pack of rattlers
for Sunday night service.
Preacher Thomas takes them out
when the spirit is fever pitch
and three or four people
who think they're right with the Lord
let them crawl across their arms
and pray in gusting whispers
as the creatures try to find a way out.
Randal lives out past the grove
with his company of reptiles.
He walks among the cages and aquariums
making notes in a ledger.
He sells one now and then,
just so they know he can.

CHICKEN DINNER

They've been down by the creek,
four generations, wild as quail.

Milo hands me the 16 gauge double
and we head across the pasture.

How come a fox or a coyote
hasn't got 'em?

Seems like the ones that could roost
are the ones to survive.
They ain't henhouse chickens anymore.

A shaggy old mare comes up
and Milo feeds it half an apple.
Two calves over by the barn.

Afternoon light slants into the trees.
Two birds flush, startle me.
Told you they was wild.

We walk the creek willows,
tall grass and blackberry.
Another flushes
I pull down on it,
it crumples to the ground.
and Beetle, Milo's hound, fetches.
Mostly Rhode Island Red
with some white speckles.

I look up at half a dozen
splotches of color
perched in the alder and ash
three or four breeds mixed in.

Let's get one more.
They ain't as plump as store bought.

IT WAS THEN

It was evening when I took the shotgun out
to the little bluff behind our house
overlooking the river where ducks flew
with such speed as to bring night in their rush.
I would try to kill one
but didn't.

It was then I looked down at the small tree
that grew in the shallow dirt for many years
only to reach the level of my knees when I saw
two rattlesnakes entwined in the cradle of its branches.
Something ancient raised my arms
and I fired.

LOUIE

Most of us had arrived
on some late wave
of westward expansion—
Scotch-Irish, Scandinavian,
German and mongrel pup,
coming by way of Oklahoma
or Arkansas, in Mormon dust,
through Humboldt dreams,
Idaho mines and Wyoming sheep,
praying for rain on some dryland farm
where you were lucky to get a chokecherry crop.
But here we were, offspring holding our own
against each other and these nomadic feet.
Except for Louie. It's like he arrived last year.
Italian. His papa ran a corner grocery
where salami swung on the garlic air
and cheeses sat like Buddhas
on the crowded counter.
At home his mama kept a pot of spaghetti sauce
on the back of the stove.
When Louie and I came home from hunting
or fishing or rummaging the wild hills
we'd drop a squirrel or rabbit or salmon cheeks
into the red mire. On a starving Thursday
I would sit down to their noodles,
listen to their chatter and taste
a wonder I never got at home.

DAPHNE

Daphne arrived at her grandmother's
down the road from us the summer I was seventeen.
I heard that it was to get her away from bad influences
somewhere in the source of all bad influences (California).
She found me within a month.
She talked about Ray Charles and the Beach Boys.
The first time I kissed her I knew
that some of those influences had come along with her.
There was no push on my part when she pulled me
on top of her on the bench seat of my father's pickup.
What rang in one ear, thank goodness,
was the voice of our health teacher,
who taught us precious little else, saying,
"Some of you boys are going to be daddies
before you graduate."
And, "You older boys remember 15 will get you 20."

YOUNG BUCK

The young buck is back this year,
alone. The doe, his mother,
the one with a game hind leg,
is absent. I imagine the skin
pulling free of her ribcage
where she lay among the oak and thistle
across Meyer Road and him visiting her
less and less as summer turns.
His horns are forked this year;
he leaps the fence with ease.

SNAKE ROAD

There's a hammer on the floor
sliding on sharp curves.
A shovel plays hockey with beer cans
in the pickup bed,
goal posts changing down the snake road.
What you don't understand
goes better with speed—
feeling the weight of inertia,
the rev and pull of a good engine,
almost in control.
I'm driving into a foreign land.
Gravel flies as I ride the ridges
past everything I know.

III

HALF A MILE

The tips of Michael's fingers
are bright pink under the cold water.
His hands disappearing and reappearing
between his mama's at the rest stop faucet
off the interstate, half a mile from Coe Road
where they get baloney and bread and milk
and cookies on a good day.
She keeps him close where they sit
with the cardboard sign, "Anything Helps."
She's got this sad look and the kid.
He runs around in his bib overalls,
arms scratched up from the blackberries
back where they sleep.
A dollar, a five, a couple of quarters.
He laughs and chases a squirrel.
A salesman offers her twenty
and they go past the fence.
It doesn't take long.
He zips up. "You're a real pro, huh?"
She mutters.
Michael mimics mama spitting in the weeds.

VACANT LOT

It was just a vacant lot
and the neighbor's dogs,
a bitch with mostly grown pups
that circled me.
I moved cautiously,
they moved, circling, with me.
I held a hand in back
and talked in tones
a pet would know
but their ears were flat,
their eyes glistened,
teeth bared.
One took a quick piece of my hand.
I spun, snarled, kicking out.
They moved back a step
and circled.
They were on a wild plain
assessing whether they could take this animal down,
rip its throat out, eat its guts.
I sidled to the neighbor's door
just a few yards away,
an oasis on a familiar continent.
Stitches closed the wound
but not the hole in time.

NOWHERE TO HIDE

Music comes down Seventh Street
close and fierce
blowing names off signs,
jumping into people's blood.
It is like fire,
the closer it gets
the more uncomfortable you feel.
There is no sweet harmony
in these juicy notes, no.
There are no jive gimmicks,
no marching, waltzing, sashaying,
two-stepping, chanting, Lindy Hopping.
No syncopated invitation, no.
It is born of clanging metal and gunfire,
trashcans banging down alleys,
cries of desperation in back rooms,
bedrooms and board rooms.
It is pain singing.

IT'S A PARADE

It's a parade,
seven of them
strung over half a block,
three crying,
two looking proper
and embarrassed,
one mad as hell
pulling a wagon,
black bags bulging with clothes
and maybe some toys.
And the last one
zigzags across lawns
and driveways
that aren't fenced.
He hoots and dashes
under sprinklers,
comes to stare at my porch
and make love-eyes at my bicycle.
His mama just keeps walking,
every now and then
calling over her shoulder
Leroy get out of that yard,
come on now
we ain't got all day.

LOOKING FOR SOME ADVANTAGE

Talk went around the room
burnishing bloodlines,
propping up their folks,
saying how their heritage
dripped pure as new honey.

I don't know about them
but many of my ancestors
were bigots, ne'er-do-wells,
and poor earth scratchers
looking for some advantage.

They didn't move all the damn time
for their health, they were looking
to trade a nag for a better horse,
maybe get a strong young man
to marry that frizzy-haired daughter.

If it could be drawn
the map of my genealogy
would look like a diagram
of colliding electrons.

A WALK TO THE RIVER

Sooner or later
you have to save your life:
no matter the decisions
you have to abandon,
the people you walk away from,
the guilt-driving looks
and pointing fingers.
It may be raining
when you walk to the river
and throw the ring
into the swiftest current.
The rain will not care
if it is the ring
or you.

DRY DAY

The lights of the roadhouse are turned off.
Two men and a woman sit at a table out back.
Four Foosball fanatics still whap the cork around
by the parking lot light through the back window.
We hear the squeal of brakes, the wheeze
of a hot engine, the thump of closing car doors,
pounding on the front door.
Jesse looks around the corner, "It's them Unruh boys."
We all poke our heads around
and there's a twenty-year-old pink Lincoln parked
half In the road, half in the gravel lot,
steaming and settling like a worn out nag,
lights shining cockeyed across the road.
Jeffery Unruh is pissing on the center line.
Billy Unruh spots us, "How do we get some goddamned beer,
we're dry as two dead birds." We just watch.
The barkeep puts a six-pack in a bag and hands it out the door.
"That'll be six bucks," he says.
Billy is fumbling in his pockets.
"I got three."
"That'll do. Now get the fuck out of here."
The Unruhs weave back to the car and jump at it
as if the Lincoln was the one that was moving.
The engine fires on the second try and they throw gravel
and sort of hop on the pavement.
"Christ," says the barkeep. "I suppose I should call the sheriff."
Jesse answers. "Maybe the state police and the National Guard."
Nobody makes a move.
Then there's the thwack of a Foosball hitting home.

POD 9

First thing you notice
is that everything is hard.
The blue-gray paint
on the poured concrete floors
and walls, the formed beds
jutting from those walls
with three inch foam pads,
the metal doors,
the stainless steel commode,
the voices that say sit down
or stand up or go there,
the cleaner smell
mixed with sweat
and pans full of stuff
cooking in the basement.
When you close your eyes
it is never dark.
The last thing you notice
is the banging rhythm
of your pulse.

WET SHOES

The river swells,
mud and debris
wash down
from scoured hills,
second growth fir
holding on.
Rainwater swirls
around the footing
of the new jail,
a concrete edifice,
three stories
and a basement
just off downtown.
Deborah Jean waits
at the outer door
in wet shoes,
then she waits
at the inner door,
the one someone
somewhere operates
like magic,
then waits in the little room
off the medium security pod
to look into the eyes
of someone she used to know.

A MARRIAGE

On a night like any other
he stood on a stool
to fix the curtain
and Parkinson's pulled
him back to the floor
and the not-quite-oblivion
of dying, the crack-neck
downward stop by the stove,
people rushing
and him looking out
at the legs, familiar voices
floating in the air above him
knowing that one voice
was half concern and half hoping
he would end here and she could
be free, at the same time
she would never be free
and to be cut loose from him
being carted to the ambulance
would mean she was too old
to do the things she longed to do
thirty years ago when she learned
to blame him and gave him that blame
with a dose of ridicule for the month
she went away,
until she came back
and he took her back
and nothing changed but the rut
as it deepened and now she follows
in the car behind flashing lights
through a darkness that will soon
take them both.

SUNSET

When the blood-red trader's moon
slips into midnight bay
brants dance the scumming tide
and pirouette on the crab-back dream.
Ship-heavy clouds drift the hour
as saw teeth devour the shadow trees.

Between time and time there is a crack,
as wide as twilight, as thin as pain,
running through the hills
as sheep ring their white bells
you and I search for circles
in the moor of lines.

FIGHTING

At lunchtime they would square off,
off campus, in back of Lenny's,
the only hamburger joint in the neighborhood.
It was bare knuckles, standup fighting—
no low blows or kicking, no funny business,
no refs either.
This wasn't third-graders poking bony ribs.
It was the first time I saw how a knuckle
could tear the flesh of a face.
They usually didn't last more than five minutes
and the same pairs never fought twice.
Three years later I would get my turn
in an alley where there were no rules
and innocence was punished
with a kick to the head.

I would take my lack of skill to Basic Training
the following year, charging through the bayonet range
yelling, "Kill. Kill. Kill. Kill. Kill."
As many times as necessary.
We battered each other with pugil sticks,
rising from the dust and grit to fight again.
Three years later in a convoy of green trucks
I looked in the rearview mirror
as my face opened
to see maggots busy inside.

FORT LEWIS, 1967

The enlisted men's bar,
a quarter in the jukebox
and the chorus rises,
"We all live in a yellow submarine..."
absurd beyond absurd
in the beery air.

National Guard, Reserve, drafted
and enlisted voice the crazy trap
we find ourselves in.

The wheel spins, the needle clicks,
whose number will be called this time?
"and we lived beneath the waves..."

What century are we in?
Have we invaded Persia?
Will we massacre Cheyenne tomorrow?
"every one of us has all we need..."

There is a brief still moment,
then someone drops in another quarter
"We all live in a yellow submarine..."
and we hold on for the dive.

TRAINING

Evil is a companion
on the machine gun range,
the chug of twisting rounds,
the human silhouettes cut in half.
It talks to me while I slowly become numb.
In the dark, one to the other,
holding the strap in front,
a step away from lost,
we are trained to trust
the voice that lies with every word.
I slide down the human scale
to the ooze at the bottom
where dying and killing melt into one.
It is a whisper. It seeps into the pores.
It creates its own gravity.
It will take a lifetime to replace.

FOUR BOYS FROM KENTUCKY

They could not dream of such meanness.
They just went where they were told
because they were taught to obey
their elders, their betters,
and God knows these people with bars
on their collars or stripes on their sleeves
certainly thought they were better.
They did their best to run faster,
shoot better, saying "Yes, Sergeant!"
while staring at the dirt under their noses,
looking after each other.
There was a decency that refused
to be kicked out of them. It couldn't
be killed or covered over thick enough
to be permanently silent.
So six weeks left in their tour,
in the exhaustion, smoke and numbness,
when they were told to kill a family
in a little house on the edge of nowhere,
they said they couldn't do that.
They said so quietly, respectfully,
but solid as a rock, no.
They were threatened, pulled off the line
and told they would be court-martialed.
They didn't say a word.
They shipped out two weeks early,
mustered out and went home.
They went back to the mills and mines
and fields and families
and never talked about it.

BURNING SALT

The smell of burning salt
drifted from the altar
across broken pews
out into the jungle.
Someone came every morning
and started a little fire,
lighted incense.
Later, when the fire turned to coals,
an old man would bring salt.
We don't know why.
No one seems to care.
The monkeys who chatter
and hang in the windows
claim there used to be fruit
in an ebony bowl.

BUGS

You can take them into the woods.
You can take them on the four lane.
You can wrap them in sheets
and throw them in a pit
where the snakes of your childhood
writhe and threaten.
You carry them to the jungle
or the desert or a mud house
where the people want to kill you.
You come home
and run down streets
hoping you can outrun them
but there is a swarm following you
and they can fly faster than you can run.
It doesn't matter if one dies
there are always more.
You speed up, you slow down.
You're just another joker
looking for a way to kill
them fucking bugs.

2:30 A.M.

There is no festival,
no party, no celebration.
No, this is a night-watch
two-thirds to five-fifths drunk.
Bars closed, we meet at the Pine Café
across from the shuttered mill
and lean on our separate stools
toward greasy hash browns
and coffee we hope will float us
to a room where the past is dead,
at least for an hour or two.
Some search the dark for a face
that will still the loneliness,
sculling a river of wine,
shouting to the echoes.
Some will lie in the car seat
in a ditch
on the way somewhere,
too cold to live
warm enough not to die.

SOME CALL IT SERVICE

First, you believe the lie
or most of it,
or you're shoved from behind
by someone who pretends to.
You get trained
like a dog.
You form a pack
ready to circle.
You run until running
takes you up a ramp,
then you fall running
into fire, until fire becomes
nothing but the blur of sun.
You become the scorched air.
You dance with death by day
and shadows at night.
You become the dirt.
You go home
and want to break things.
You break.
You pick up the pieces
one by one
and lay them in the street
where traffic will pulverize them.
Sooner or later you might feel it.

MUCH IMPROVED

Hardly anyone dies of typhoid fever
anymore. We can send our sons to war
without complaint. Lice are quickly dispatched
and no one freezes to death.
We have piles of antibiotics.
The broadsword wounded aren't left
in the field to die with others rotting around them.
Of course there are more bombs and bullets
but morphine is readily available.
We can usually save a soldier whose limb
is blown off.
Yes, things are much improved.
We can send more daughters up to the front.
They have the right.
Soldiering is still a good option for the poor.
We're working on pills for madness,
more medications to calm the nerves
and we'll get a handle on this suicide business,
yes we will.

MEETING

"Are you one of them?"
Doug levels the accusation with a soup spoon
pointed at my chest. The collar of his flannel shirt
is separating, his cowlick spreads gray above
a rounded forehead, his clothes are unwashed.
I remember us riding recklessly through the countryside,
the Vietnam War hounding us, betrayal in the back seat,
sailing over railroad tracks, around impossible detours.
Until I broke.
I stood in the basement of the National Guard armory,
raised my right hand and repeated words
the sergeant read from a gray card.
Doug disappeared after that, like a coyote
fading into the undergrowth.
Thirty-two years later, he's eating egg flower soup,
looking slightly mischievous in tatters.
"The stars still come out at night," I reply.

MY BROTHER WAS A MOUSE

My brother was a mouse
in a garden of mice.

His pistol was polished and clean.

The number he chanted
had three digits
and rang among the catalpa leaves.

When they came for him
he put on the uniform
and marched away.

As fleas on a beagle
were their numbers.

It was a long time
before he came home
impaled on a curtain rod.

JUST AFTER DARK

The frogs started up this week.
Their chorus from dips and pools
just after dark reassuring us
that spring is happening again.
They peeped on the day I boarded a Greyhound
for Fort Lewis, and again when my friend Lester
left for Vietnam. It was August and dry
when I returned and it was November
when they brought Lester back.
I go to see him on Thursdays at the home.
Sometimes he knows me,
sometimes he looks through me.
The frogs are out there now,
doing their job.

YOURS, MINE AND OURS

They sit on the porch
talking a language
fit for a hot afternoon.

"You seen Hollister's boy?"
"Yes I have."

Grasshoppers dance in the yard.

"That war messed him up good."
"That it did."

The smell of pine and sweat lay in the air.

"They say he busted up Shorty's tavern last night."
"I heard."

One of the Sutter boys rides by on a rusty bike.

"He should do more fishing and less fighting."
"That's true. And if he survives another year or two he
might."

A dust devil travels the field across the road.

"Took us a while, with our war."
"Yes it did."

HAMMER MAN

"You can't eat the stars,"
he said as he slammed the three pound hammer
on the sixteen penny nail.
We were building low-end houses
on the back road to paradise, 1968.
I was carrying two-by-fours
to the wall I was framing.
"You can eat the moon,
but not the stars," he continued.
"What the hell are you talking about?"
I dropped the two-by-fours
on the subfloor planking
Wendell had jammed into place.
He started to hum and kept hammering.

I was eating a sandwich in the shade
when the boss slid down beside me.
He popped open a black lunch box.
"Don't mind Wendell," he said.
"He's out there a ways," I said.
"He's got his reasons.
I've pried a few stories out of him.
He was a gas truck driver on the Burma Road
during World War II.
He can't figure out why he's still alive,
but he can drive nails like John Henry."

We chewed and looked across lumber to a pile of gravel.
"During the war they worked in small crews.
He came in late and drunk one night
tried to sleep on his cot but he was so drunk
it kept bucking him off.
So he crawled into a corner and passed out.

Next morning he woke to find
everybody but him had their throats cut.
He lived in terror long enough
that something came loose in his head."
That afternoon I listened to Wendell's hammer
banging in nails like a slow machine gun
as I framed walls behind him.

V

HOUSE AT FINN CREEK

It was two-walled
but barely.
If there was newspaper insulation
I would be surprised.
The inside walls would sweat in winter,
mildew and blackberries holding
the roof in place.
We kept four chickens
in a ten foot pen out back
until skunks or possums,
some creature in the dark
tore them apart.
There was a little airtight stove
that almost heated the place,
near melting against the cold.
The creek out back was a rat run
but our big orange tom
took care of them with great satisfaction.
The rent fit my wages
and we lived there four years
scratching a garden,
sparking each other,
green as saplings.

ENDEAVOR

The stink is on,
coming from the marsh
where runoff drains
into old mill waste
that overlays the sewers
from pioneer days.

Further out the clams
keep going and crabs
clack their hungry dance
along the bay bed.
Tourists bob in little boats,
fish lines and crab pots
strung between jetty rocks
and the channel.

A grandpa breath breeze
slings up along the road
where we're selling handmade birdhouses
and genuine kelp pickles.
It's a fine day for commerce.

BLESSING AT THE BAY FRONT CAFÉ

You can't tell she is a she
in the black suit purchased in 1948,
coming out of the wind off highway 101
intently gliding in like a Marx brother
cued to the next scene.

She turns from the piano bench,
nods to us as we grow silent.
She holds her delicate hands over the keys
in the drift of garlic, butter and wine
then plunges into Rachmaninoff.

Cuff links flash from black sleeves,
hair divided into two dark clusters
dyed and slicked down,
hands fluttering like mad sparrows
in a Russian dream.

Half an hour, an hour, a half eaten meal,
rain outside turns to snow, a samovar
glows in the corner, we speak of revolution.
No cars or log trucks pass while she plays.
Fish barely fin the water in Isthmus Slough.

You never know when she'll come,
no one does, but we wait and hope
it's our moment she blesses.
We smile and applaud her humble exit,
a hint of Bay Rum cologne left behind.

DOWNSTREAM

There were moments when I was fearless
moving down an unseen channel,
at home in the nameless water
that carried me.

Forgive me for not being able to say
where I was going. I didn't know.
The stars reflected in dark pools
and I had to wade among them.

WARD B, 10:15 P.M.

We are making rounds, checking bodies.
We reposition a few, turn a head, change diapers.
No babies here, some are teenagers,
others older, approaching death.
Age fades to meaninglessness
among these beds. Some have sat
in wheelchairs during the day,
some moved from bed to vinyl chair
and back, fed from lap boards,
touched when necessary.
Our words slip around them,
oscillations and fibers of meaning
sift over translucent skin and unwashed hair.
Our worlds orbit the same genetic sun,
but we remain strangers.
Only Wally, crazy Wally, will scoop up
one of these ruined bodies,
legs and arms akimbo,
and waltz down the hall
through other wards and back
singing, "You're an angel baby,
my angel baby mine.
Come fly with me to the moon,
angel baby mine."
We finish with diapers
and make one last bed check
where Claudia's eyes watch me
with all the blue there is.

THE OLD NEIGHBORHOOD

Sometimes I understand
that this self I form
and reform daily
is like paint on a house.

The rooms are full of air
and singing and mouse droppings.

Sometimes I see
through the dusty,
fly-specked window
a wheeling galaxy.

I tend a garden
in that sky.

I DON'T BELIEVE

I don't believe much in believing.

But if I were to believe something
it would be that we are electromagnetic fields
at play on the quantum stage.

I would believe that we are light
in jackets of flesh stitched together
with probability waves.

I would believe that awareness
is the shimmer of dancing particles,
knowing and being one.

If I were to believe anything.

ORDINARY GRAVITY

Some say they see angels at the event horizon;
others, that anything we see is a projection,
a hologram somehow created by us
to step into and believe.

The old scenarios of judgment, heaven and hellfire
taught us about symbols, that we get wisdom aslant.
We look for soul in the great karmic tides,
in the river that never ceases to run,
in the dust left by elephant gods.

For those who have touched the cold clay
of their mother or killed and slaughtered a calf
there is a darkness no lens can pierce.

Some are satisfied knowing that our molecules
will go on to enrich the thin life of this planet
held in the vast sky that tells us everything
in a language we are just beginning to learn.

NOW

It's not just our eyes.
It's the eyes of the dinosaur,
the trilobite, the spark dash
of fish hunting ancient seas,
the stone whispers running
under our feet, the stilled
motion of a hand
bringing quiet to a child.
It's the song sung by quanta
across our vein of stars.
It's today and always.
It's you and me.

NIGHT TALK

Outside the halo of firelight
bones rattle in the long dark,
shadows dance,
trees reach.

Mountain cradle,
horizon to horizon
the sky lurid with stars—
a midnight wider than wise.

Incubation in the shallow dirt
on this planet,
we build our schemes
on the great sea of indifference.

Trepidation as we stare
past the place of questions,
a glimpse of that which circles us
as we revolve.

We stir the embers
and tell each other stories
we almost believe—
lay meaning in the ashes.

The original loneliness:
we carry it with the first
glimmer of consciousness
in that part of our brain that howls.

COMING HOME

The other night
in a motel
on the road home
the heavy footfalls,
then the banging
headboard at midnight
reminded me that we
are quiet love makers,
slow pleasure givers,
and prefer daylight,
touching the moon
at midday.

BLACKBERRY JAM

All the summers melt together
as the green river mixes
with a hot blackberry wind
and there is no other season,
no other life.
Clusters of fruit hang like gifts.
All you have to do
is brave the thorns.

At home we strain seeds
from the bubbling mass.
Not all of them,
there will be surprise lumps
for the smooth January taste.
We smear jam on cheeks
and lips and tongues
and hold each other with
wounded arms.

OCTOBER LEAVES

Sweetgum leaves fall to the desperate lawn.
The porch needs sweeping.
I sit in the old wicker chair
watching ducks come and go
on the pond.

These turning leaves carry me
to a time when I discovered a wild freedom.
That first year in college, after selling band instruments
and working the hospital swing shift,
leaving parents who saw college as a foreign land
and their work world, that sore back labor world,
where if you wanted to eat you cut timber,
hauled logs, stacked lumber or sold it;
that world where you bucked hay bales
and picked beans or fruit, always for someone else.
And here I was with a life outrageously open
in drifts of campus maple leaves,
exuberance dancing in my blood.
Flying and falling in each startling moment.
How does one welcome such a guest?
What does one do?

Freedom is not easily held onto,
but I kept a little piece in my pocket
past the rules and requirements,
past basic training and mistakes in loving
for that time I would recognize it
offered on the wind.

Mallards arrive over the rooftop
and settle on the water.

ACKNOWLEDGMENTS

These poems originally appeared in, or were accepted at, the following publications, sometimes in an earlier version.

Apeiron Review: "Fighting"

Badlands Literary Journal: "Looking for Some Advantage," "Lower River Road," "A Walk to the River"

Blue Collar Review: "Nowhere to Hide"

The Cape Rock: "Some Call it Service"

Cascadia Review: "Endeavor," "Night Talk," "Vacant Lot," "Ward B, 10:15 P.M."

Cloudbank: "Four Boys From Kentucky," "The Game"

Cobra Lily Review: "Snake Road"

Common Ground Review: "Second Week of School"

Fennel Stalk: "Sunset"

Hubbub: "Burning Salt," "Hammer Man"

Jefferson Journal: "Blackberry Jam"

Mobius: The Journal of Social Change: "Much Improved"

Passager: "Beast of Burden," "Yours, Mine and Ours"

Permafrost: "Half a Mile"

Pinyon: "Dry Day," "Snake Country"

Poetry Pacific: "2:30 A.M.," "Bugs,"

Ponder Review: "It Was Then," "Meeting"

Red River Review: "Wet Shoes"

San Pedro River Review: "Blessing at the Bay Front Café"

Sisyphus: "I Don't Believe"

Slant: "Lesson"

So It Goes: The Literary Journal of the Kurt Vonnegut Museum and Library: "Just After Dark"

Song of the San Joaquin Quarterly: "Grandpa Cramer's Last Speech"

Spank the Carp: "A Marriage," "The Old Neighborhood"

Steam Ticket: "It's a Parade"

StringTown Magazine: "Keith"

Talking River: "My Brother Was a Mouse"

Turtle Island Quarterly: "Downstream," "Young Buck," "Father's People"

Westview: "Bridge Across"

Willawaw Journal: "Louie"

Windfall: "House at Finn Creek," "We Didn't Tell Him We Were Neighbors"

ZYZZYVA: "Now," "Ordinary Gravity"

"Father's People," was included in the chapbook *River of Solace*, an Editor's Choice Chapbook Award from *Turtle Island Quarterly,* Flowstone Press.

Thank you to Dorothy for everything.

Also to Airlie editors: Kelly Terwilliger, Tim Whitsel, Jon Boisvert, Jessica Mehta, José Araguz, Jennifer Perrine, Amelia Díaz Ettinger. Help and counsel much appreciated.

ABOUT THE PUBLISHER

Airlie Press is run by writers. A nonprofit publishing
collective, the press is dedicated to producing beautiful
and compelling books of poetry. Its mission is to offer
a shared-work publishing alternative for writers working
in the Pacific Northwest. Airlie Press is supported by
book sales and donations. All funds return to the press
for the creation of new books of poetry.

COLOPHON

The titles and poems are set throughout in Calibri, a
modern sans serif family with subtle roundings on
stems and corners. It is a humanist sans serif typeface,
known for its warmth. Commissioned by Microsoft in
2002 from Luc(as) de Groot, a German typographer
and the head of font foundry, Fontfabrik. It has received
consistent praise and is in use worldwide.